Standard Tuning
SLIDE GUITAR

by GREG KOCH

The price of this publication includes access to video online for download or streaming, using the unique code below.

To access video visit:
www.halleonard.com/mylibrary

Enter Code
2977-4075-7162-7964

ISBN 978-1-4768-1501-5

HAL•LEONARD®
CORPORATION
7777 W. BLUEMOUND RD. P.O. BOX 13819 MILWAUKEE, WI 53213

In Australia Contact:
Hal Leonard Australia Pty. Ltd.
4 Lentara Court
Cheltenham, Victoria, 3192 Australia
Email: ausadmin@halleonard.com.au

Visit Hal Leonard Online at
www.halleonard.com

Introduction

Standard Tuning Slide Guitar is a compilation of standard-tuned slide techniques accumulated by the author for over 30 years. The point of this book is to demonstrate how to play convincing blues, rock, country, and gospel-tinged slide guitar while in standard tuning by using techniques and approaches that will make you sound, at times, as though you are in other tunings, such as open E or open G. Drawing from a well of influences, from Blind Willie Johnson and Elmore James to Duane Allman and Sonny Landreth, the author will show you how to achieve some of these sounds in standard tuning and will hopefully provide ideas that inspire the development of your own style.

Things You Will Need

GUITAR

An acoustic or electric guitar will work for these lessons. Some approaches might be demonstrated with one or the other, but all of the techniques referenced can be performed on either electric or acoustic guitar.

A steel-string acoustic guitar sounds great with slide. The size of the body will affect the tone and volume of the guitar, but it is totally a matter of personal preference. The quality of the instrument should not hinder the student, as most of the classic old blues recordings like Robert Johnson's were probably done on inexpensive guitars. Although a famous picture shows him playing a Gibson L-1, many sources say he usually played a Stella or Kalamazoo and most likely recorded with one of those guitars.

A guitar with a resonator, such as a metal-bodied National or a round-necked Dobro, are often used for slide. In the days before amplification, resonators were popular guitars among bluesmen because they gave them a louder, more nasal tone, which was easier to hear than a regular acoustic guitar. They do sound great with slide, and there are many affordable options out there these days, but it is not necessary to have one to play effective acoustic slide guitar.

Electric guitars with humbucking pickups sound great when playing slide, as the thicker, louder sound of these guitars helps the notes sustain a bit better right out of the gate. Guitars with single-coil pickups will get a much glassier tone but often need the tube compression of an amp turned up a bit, or an overdrive or compression pedal, to add a little more "meat" and sustain so the notes can sing a little longer than a straight clean sound would allow.

In this day and age, there are many affordable solid-state and digital amplifiers that provide a wide variety of tones and sound good at a whisper volume. Conventional wisdom dictates that tube-powered amps will deliver the most organic tone and widest dynamic control, but it is entirely up to the player. The music doesn't care one way or the other!

The following lick is played with an acoustic guitar and then an acoustic resonator guitar so that you can hear the difference between the two.

▶ Acoustic

▶ Acoustic Resonator

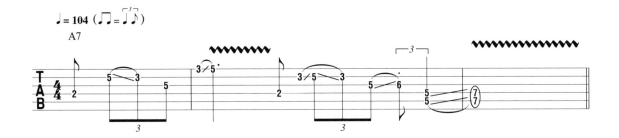

Next, I'll play the same lick using an electric guitar with humbuckers and then one with single coils, both through a tube amp; first, with a clean tone (with and without a compressor), and then with an overdriven tone.

▶ Electric with Humbuckers – Clean

▶ Electric with Humbuckers – Clean with Compressor

▶ Electric with Humbuckers – Overdrive

▶ Electric with Single Coils – Clean

▶ Electric with Single Coils – Clean with Compressor

▶ Electric with Single Coils – Overdrive

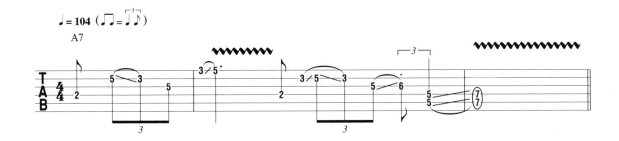

No special setup is necessary; although, if the action on your guitar is really low, it may be very difficult to prevent the slide from "bottoming out" on the fretboard.

SLIDE

This is entirely a matter of personal preference, although here are some things to consider: glass slides have a mellower, rounder tone but, depending on the thickness of the glass, you have to apply more pressure with your fretting hand to get the desired volume and attack—and glass breaks at the most inopportune times. Steel or brass slides have a brighter tone than glass and generate loud, defined notes more easily, although they lack a bit of the dynamic control and warmth you get from a glass slide. Plus, you can attach metal slides to the magnet of the speaker of your amp, which is a good way to keep track of them! Chances are, you will end up playing all the various types of slides when different opportunities present themselves.

The following is a short excerpt to show the difference between glass and metal slides on electric guitar.

 Glass Slide

 Metal Slide

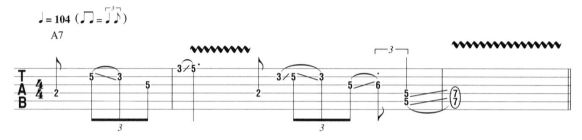

Which Finger to Use for Playing Slide?

Again, this is totally a matter of personal preference and there is no right or wrong answer. The author currently enjoys playing slide on the third finger of his slide hand. This seems to allow for greater control in terms of consistent intonation, vibrato, and inflection, but wearing the slide on this finger makes it a little more difficult to play chords and fretted notes with your other fingers.

Wearing the slide on the pinky finger of your slide hand certainly allows you the most freedom to use your other fingers to play chords and other fretted notes, but the pinky is not the strongest of the phalanges and, as a result, it's a little harder to control intonation, vibrato, and inflection when playing slide.

The middle finger is another excellent option, as it allows you to use other fingers to fret and gives you good control with the slide, although it does look like you are flipping the audience "the Bird"… but, to each his own!

No matter what finger you end up using, it is a good idea to use the finger directly behind the slide to mute the strings to reduce unwanted noise. So, if you are using the slide on your middle finger, your first finger would mute the strings behind the slide; for ring-finger sliding, your middle finger would mute, and for pinky sliding, the ring finger would mute.

Pick-Hand Muting

▶ Pick-Hand Muting

You can certainly use a pick to play slide and employ the palm of your picking hand to mute strings you do not wish to hear. Many great players have done this, from Earl Hooker to Billy Gibbons. This is an effective way to play slide. However, many players opt to use no pick, instead using a fingerpicking technique that not only provides a fantastic way to mute strings, but also seems to give the player a wider dynamic range, mellower attack, and rounder-sounding tone.

The template for this pick-hand muting technique is basically this: your ring finger is designated for the high E string, middle finger for the B string, index finger for the G string, and your thumb is draped over the lower three strings. This gives the player the ability to hit specific strings while muting others. This is especially important when playing slide in standard tuning because it deadens unsympathetic notes.

Although you may use these same finger-to-string relationships to pick each string, many folks end up doing the lion's share of their picking with their thumb and first finger, especially for faster passages, but then return to the aforementioned positions.

In addition to being an excellent way to mute the strings, this style of fingerpicking also sounds great and gives the player wide dynamic control, as you can "pop" strings with more force or lightly pluck them. The following lick is played with a pick so you can hear the difference.

▶ Playing with Pick

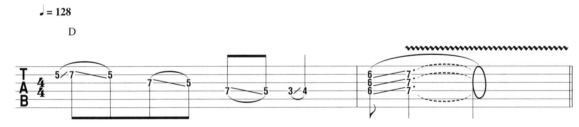

This next example shows how you can adjust the fingerpicking to allow for faster passages before returning to the initial positioning.

▶ Fingerpicking Positions

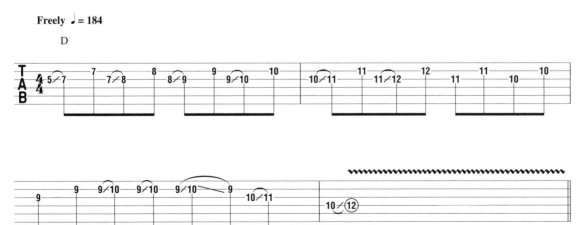

Open-Position E Blues Scale

The expressway to improvisation on a blues tune is utilizing the notes of the blues scale, so let's start with using the slide to hit the notes of the open-position E blues scale. We'll include what would be the extension position of the blues scale, going up to the fifth fret on the B and high E strings. A good way to calibrate your intonation with the slide versus your fingered notes is to run a few notes of the scale with conventional fingering and then repeat what you've played, trying to match the intonation while using the slide. Keep in mind that you need only apply as much pressure on the string with your slide to get the note to ring and that you must be over the desired fret wire (and not behind it).

 Open-Position E Blues Scale (0:00)

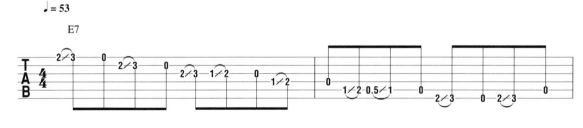

SLIDING INTO NOTES

One way to give your slide playing a bluesy flavor is to slide up to every note. The following exercise does just that. Hear how it automatically gives the scale a little more personality.

 Open-Position E Blues Scale (1:42)

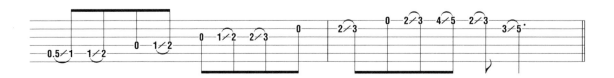

Although sliding up to notes seems to happen more often, sliding down to each note can definitely give your playing some attitude. Let's play our blues scale, sliding down to each note.

Open-Position E Blues Scale (2:33)

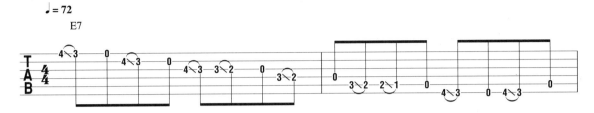

The following four licks utilize slides to go up and down to the notes for more of a bluesy flavor.

Sliding into Notes – Lick 1

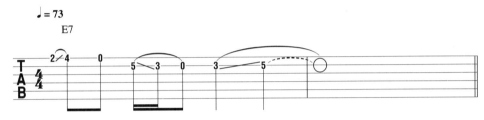

Sliding into Notes – Lick 2

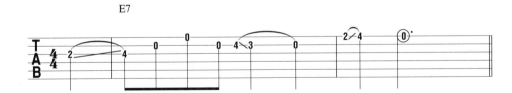

Sliding into Notes – Lick 3

Sliding into Notes – Lick 4

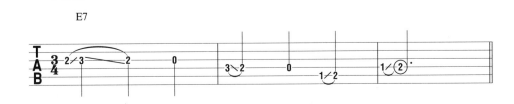

VIBRATO

Clearly, mastering vibrato with the slide is a high priority, as it is something that can have an especially visceral effect on listeners, as well as being a clear way for a player to establish his or her musical identity. Whether it is a fast, narrow vibrato or a syrupy, slow, and wide vibrato, having consistent command and good intonation is a challenge. One way to avoid intonation problems is to slide up to a note to hit the desired pitch and then add vibrato. Sometimes just aiming for a note and beginning the vibrato immediately can make the intonation a little dicey.

The vibrato itself can be achieved by keeping your wrist and hand relatively stiff while gently using your elbow to rock back and forth. The motion to get the vibrato is seemingly instigated by your fingers and wrist, but the actual motion is happening at the elbow.

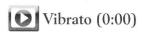 Vibrato (0:00)

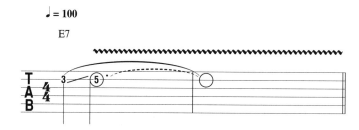

The following exercise involves sliding up to the notes of our E blues scale and then adding a fast, narrow vibrato.

 Vibrato (2:03)

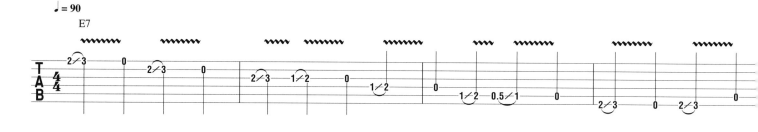

Now let's do the same thing with a slower, wider vibrato. Note that it does not require a lot of horizontal real estate to get a wider-sounding vibrato. A back-and-forth motion of about a centimeter will sound cavernous.

 Vibrato (2:32)

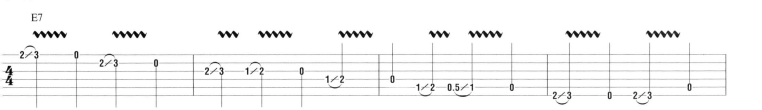

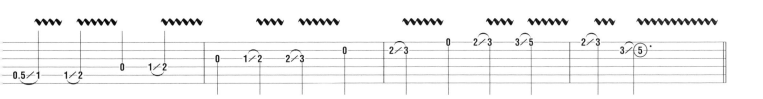

Here are a few licks using vibrato and the other things we have learned thus far:

 Vibrato – Lick 1

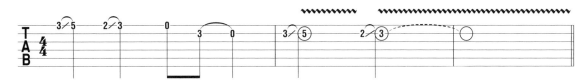

 Vibrato – Lick 2

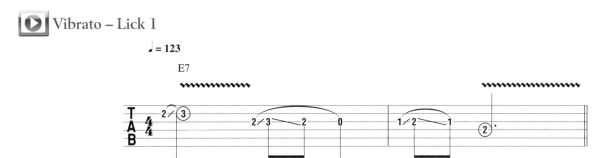

 Vibrato – Lick 3

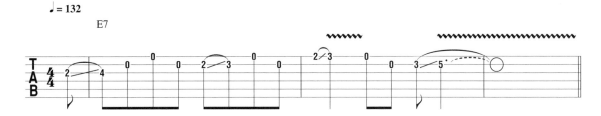

PLAYING A BLUES WITH SINGLE NOTES

The great thing about playing slide guitar is that, with an effective vibrato and some of the other nuances we've learned, you can play a blues with single notes and really hear the chord changes (if you utilize the *right* notes). The next example is two choruses of a 12-bar blues that will give you an idea of what can be done with just the information learned thus far.

 Single-Note Blues

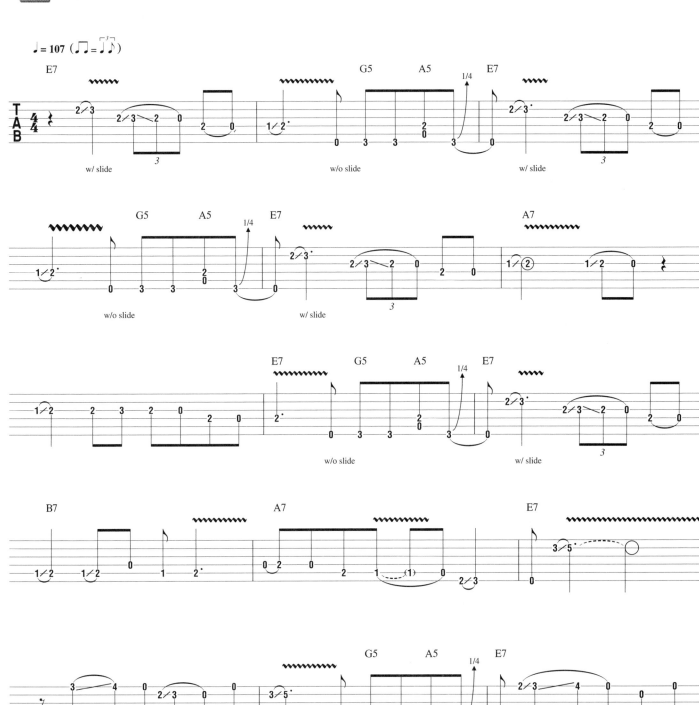

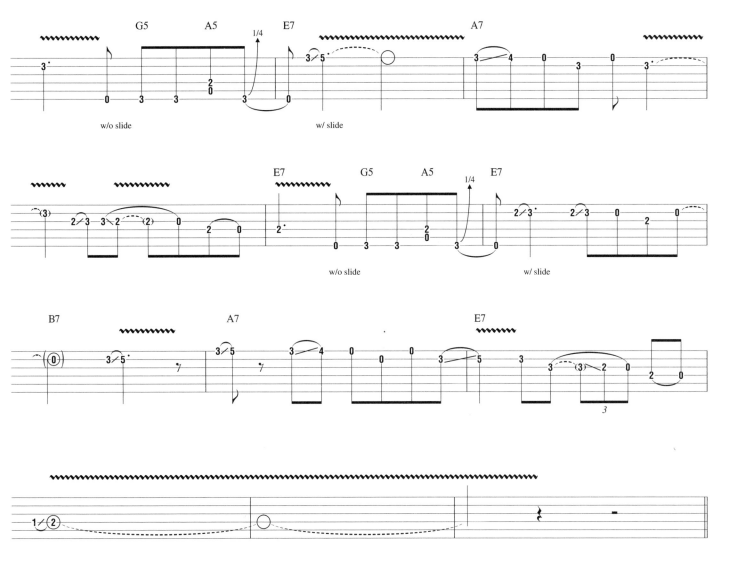

ADDING DOUBLE AND TRIPLE STOPS

When playing slide in open tunings, whereby the guitar is tuned to an open chord like E or G, you can place the slide over a desired fret and hit all the strings at once and they will spell out a major chord. When you are playing slide in standard tuning, you have to be much more careful when attempting to adhere to a given key, so you are usually confined to playing double and triple stops.

In our open position, here are some double stops for the I chord (E) in an E major blues. The first example is just hitting the A and D strings at the second fret. This double stop contains the 5th (B) on the bottom and the root (E) on the top.

Double and Triple Stops (0:00)

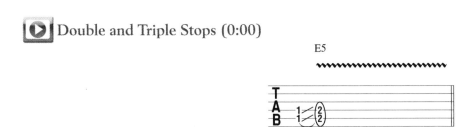

The second example is a little trickier because you are hitting the G string and the high E string at the fourth fret while simultaneously muting the B string. If you are using the fingerpicking method, this will not be a problem, but if you are using a pick, you will have to employ hybrid picking by using the pick on the G string and your middle finger on the high E string, being careful not to sound the B string. This double stop gets you the flavor of the I chord with the 5th (B) on the bottom and the 3rd (G♯) on top. If I slide up to each double stop and add a little vibrato, they sound a little more interesting.

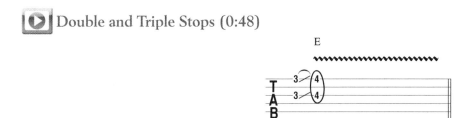

Double and Triple Stops (0:48)

To get the IV chord (A) for a blues in E, we can play a triple stop at the second fret using the slide on the D, G, and B strings. Again, I'll slide up to these notes and add a little vibrato.

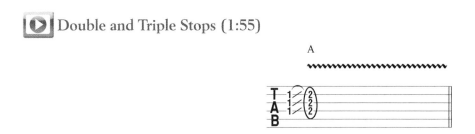

Double and Triple Stops (1:55)

For the V chord (B), we can play a triple stop at the fourth fret of the D, G, and B strings.

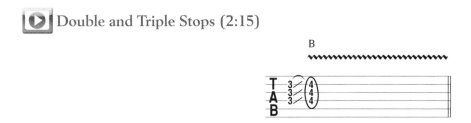

Double and Triple Stops (2:15)

The following piece is a country blues that utilizes all the things we have learned thus far. Notice how adding double and triple stops really helps spell out the chord changes and allows you to do an effective solo blues piece that sounds full and complete. You can effectively slide up or down to these double and triple stops to add a more bluesy flavor. This piece is being played on an acoustic resonator guitar.

Country Blues

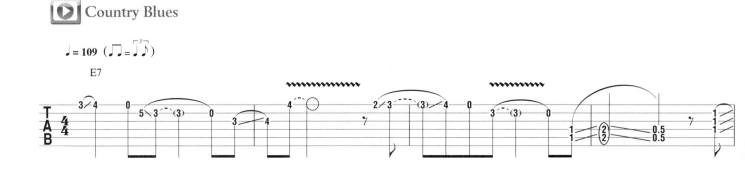

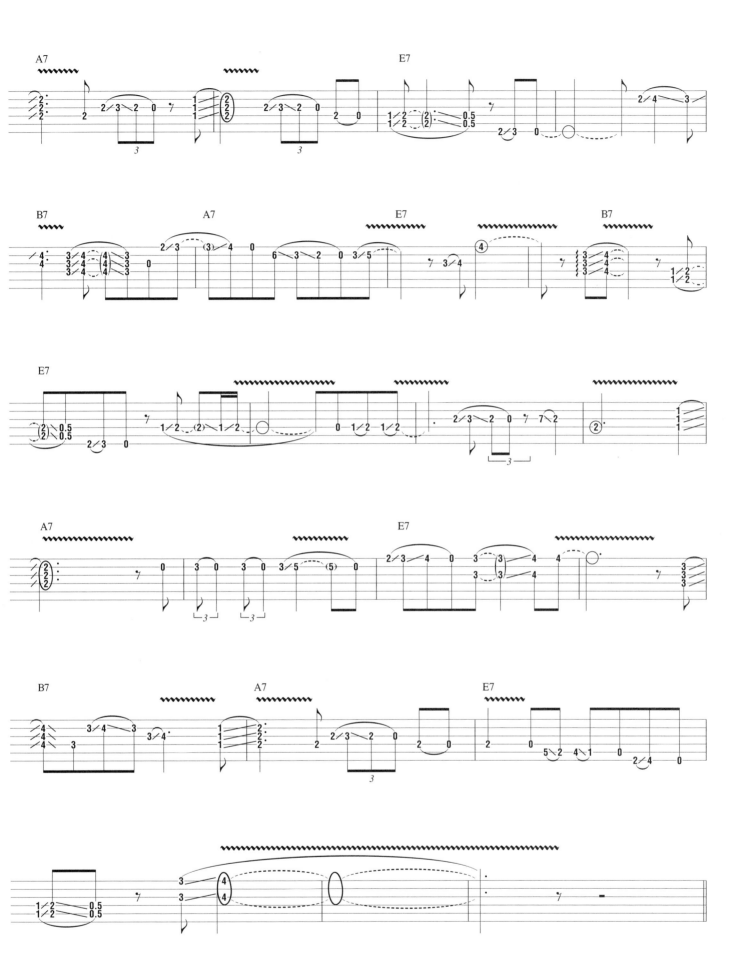

Moveable Blues Positions

To move the blues scale around the neck, it is helpful to find triple or double stops of the major I chord in the key you are playing over as a kind of "home base." We will touch on playing over minor chords later in this book, but for now, here are some exercises for identifying moveable blues-scale positions by finding sympathetic double or triple stops. These exercises sometimes cross over into multiple positions, but they provide different ways of utilizing the same notes all over the neck. Play each position by sliding up or down to each note and adding vibrato when appropriate. There will then be examples of licks for each position that will incorporate all the tools we have learned thus far.

The first position is centered on the E double stop at the fourth fret of the G and high E strings and the double stop at the second fret of the A and D strings.

Here are a few licks in this position:

 Moveable Blues Positions – Lick 1

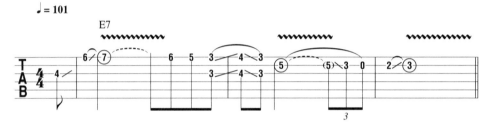

 Moveable Blues Positions – Lick 2

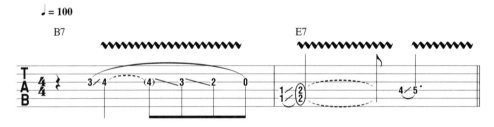

 Moveable Blues Positions – Lick 3

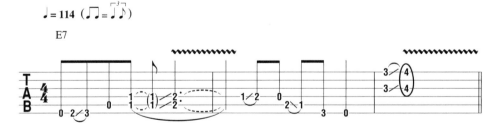

The second position is centered around the double stop at the 12th fret of the B and high E strings and the triple stop at the ninth fret of the D, G, and B strings and continues to descend, covering the length of the neck.

Here are a few licks in this position:

▶ Moveable Blues Positions – Lick 4

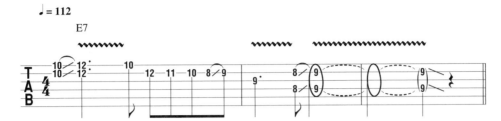

▶ Moveable Blues Positions – Lick 5

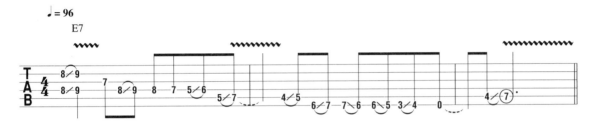

▶ Moveable Blues Positions – Lick 6

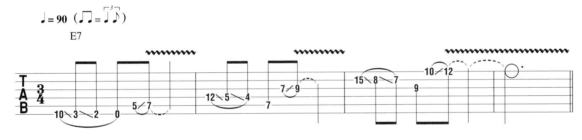

The third position also starts on the B and high E strings at the 12th fret but then proceeds to outline the E major chord around the 12th fret position, including touching on the G♯ note at the 13th fret of the G string before hitting the double stop at the 14th fret of the A and D strings.

Here are a few licks in this position:

▶ Moveable Blues Positions – Lick 7

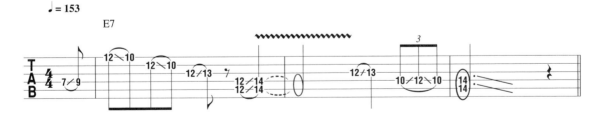

▶ Moveable Blues Positions – Lick 8

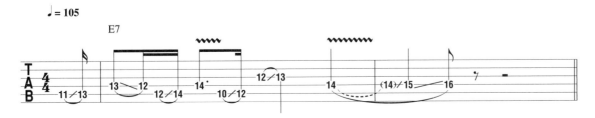

▶ Moveable Blues Positions – Lick 9

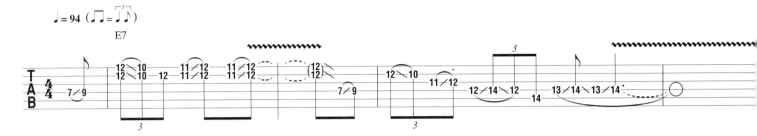

To play over the IV (A) and V (B) chords of a blues in E, we can move the positions that we played for the I (E) chord. The following examples transpose some of the exercises that we played in E to A and, in the final example, to B.

▶ Moveable Blues Positions – Lick 10

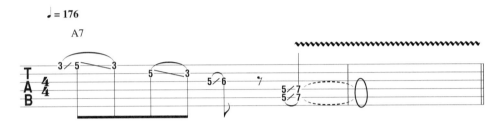

▶ Moveable Blues Positions – Lick 11

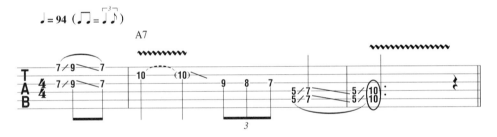

▶ Moveable Blues Positions – Lick 12

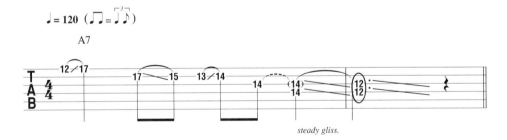

steady gliss.

▶ Moveable Blues Positions – Lick 13

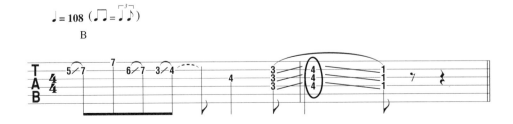

16

The following shuffle is an Elmore James-meets-Duane Allman piece using the moveable positions and some of the licks we just learned. It's played with an electric guitar, an overdriven tone, and the bridge pickup.

Shuffle in E

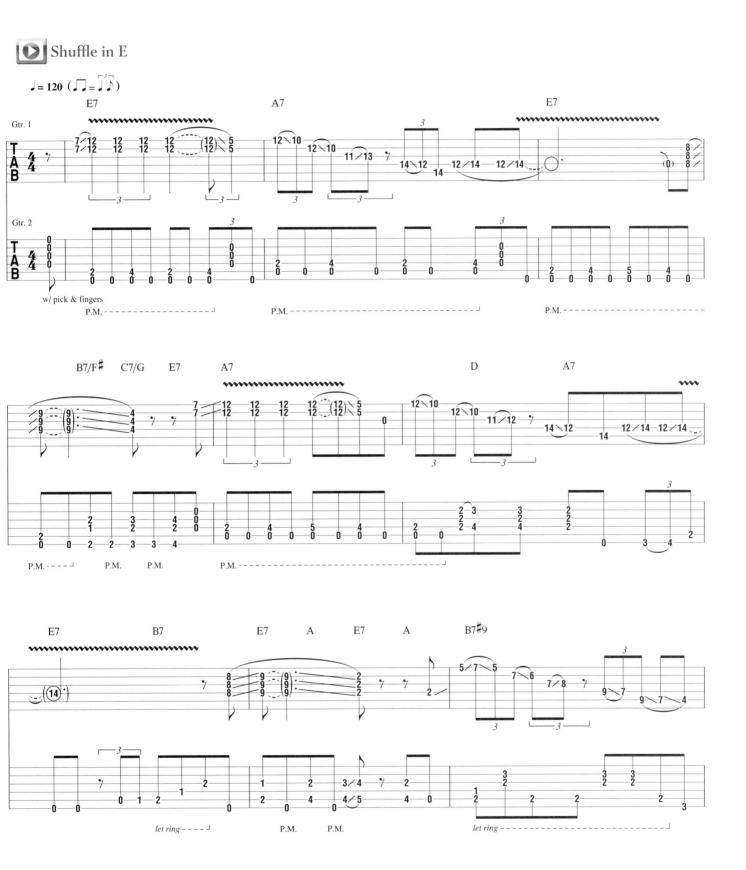

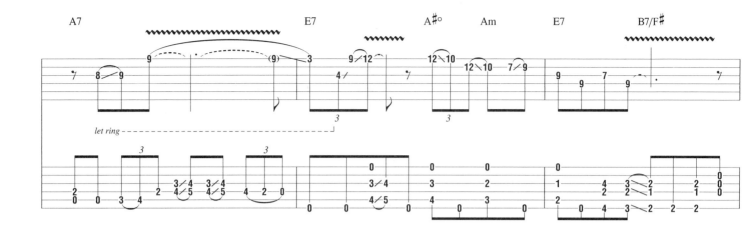

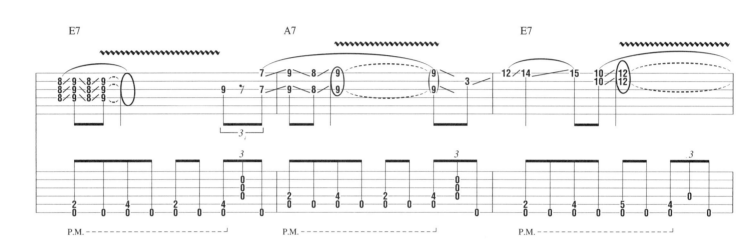

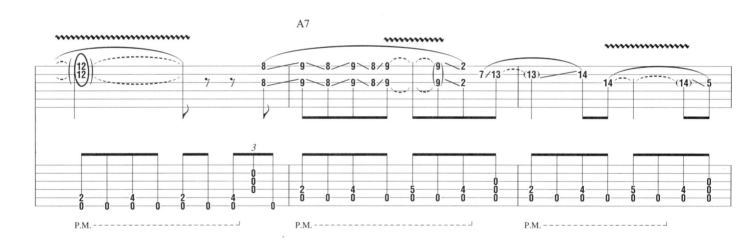

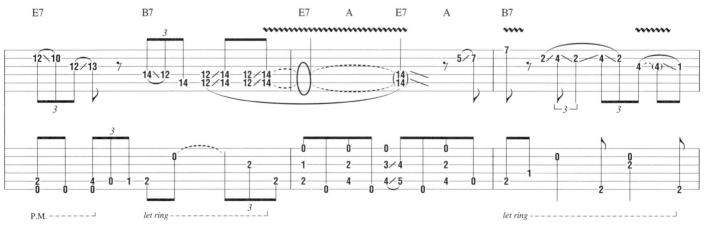

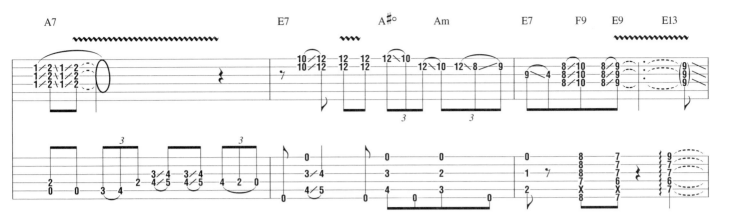

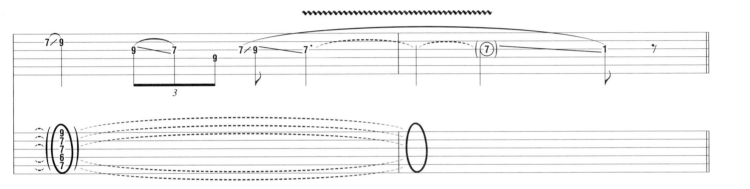

Major Pentatonic Scale with Added ♭3rd

If we took all the notes from the E blues scale but changed the root to G, we would get a G major pentatonic scale with an added ♭3rd. One of the many things that's great about playing guitar is that you can visually make connections on the neck to help you figure out what you are doing, and this is one of those times. All the scale positions we just learned for the E blues scale you can now apply to the G major pentatonic, although the notes you want to emphasize will change. This scale is great for more "major-ish"-sounding things while playing over major chords that don't have a ♭7th, although you can use it in a blues format, as well, which we will get into later. It should be noted that, like the ♭5th in the blues scale, the ♭3rd in this scale is used as a passing tone, and if you linger on it too long when improvising, it can be highly disturbing and may cause the listener to beg for resolution!

This first exercise uses the open-position G major pentatonic scale with the added ♭3rd in an ascending and descending pattern.

 Major Pentatonic with ♭3rd

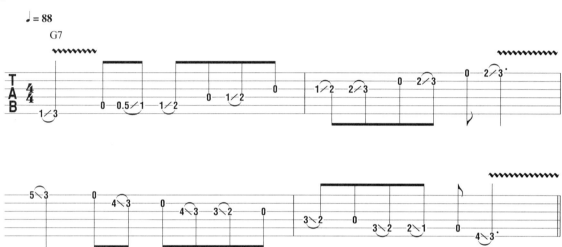

Here are a few licks using this position and the skills we've learned thus far:

 Major Pentatonic with ♭3rd – Lick 1

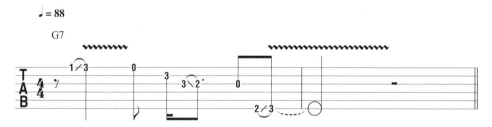

Major Pentatonic with ♭3rd – Lick 2

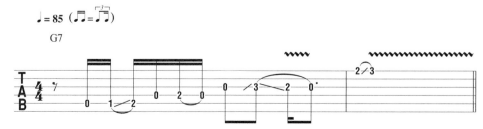

▶ Major Pentatonic with ♭3rd – Lick 3

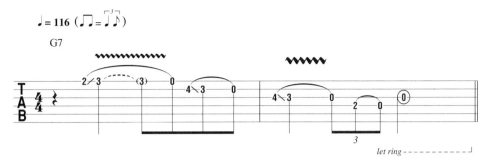

The second position is what I like to call the "pentatonic extension," which starts with the open G string of our open-position pentatonic and gives you a little more horizontal movement up the neck on the top strings.

▶ Major Pentatonic with ♭3rd Extension

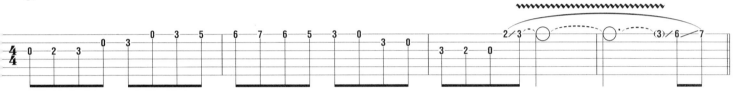

Here are a few licks using this position combined with the open position…

▶ Major Pentatonic with ♭3rd Extension – Lick 1

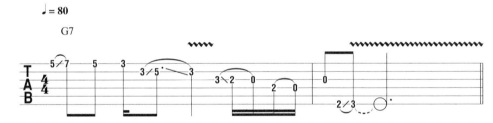

▶ Major Pentatonic with ♭3rd Extension – Lick 2

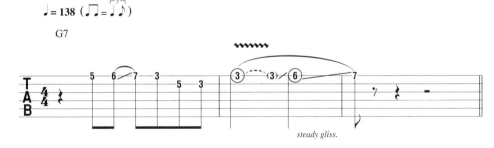

▶ Major Pentatonic with ♭3rd Extension – Lick 3

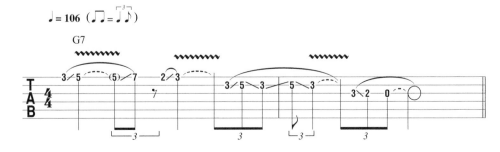

21

The fourth exercise starts with the G root at the third fret of the low E string, ascends horizontally to the G note at the 15th fret of the high E string, and then goes back down again.

▶ Major Pentatonic with ♭3rd Extension – Lick 4

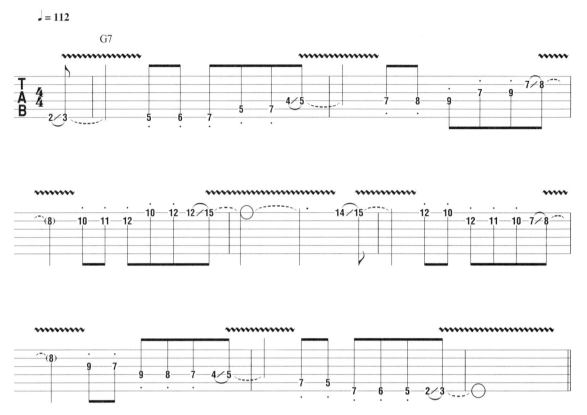

The next selection is a two-chord vamp (G to C) and we are going to employ the G major pentatonic scale and the tools in our shed that we've learned thus far, including the moveable double and triple stops that spell out the G and C chords.

▶ G Major Vamp

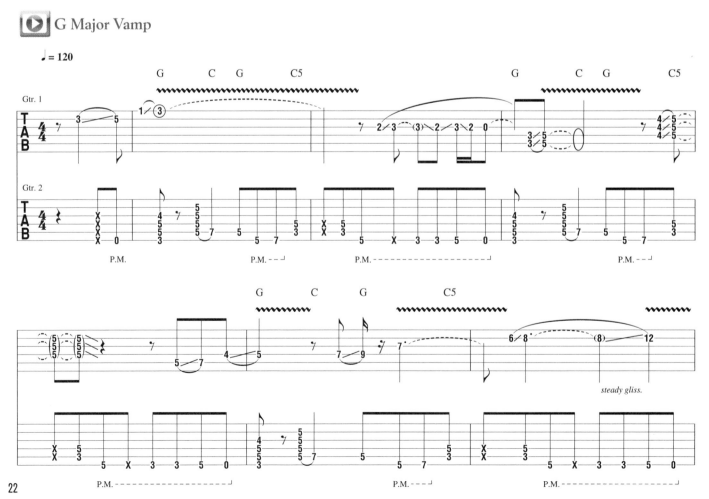

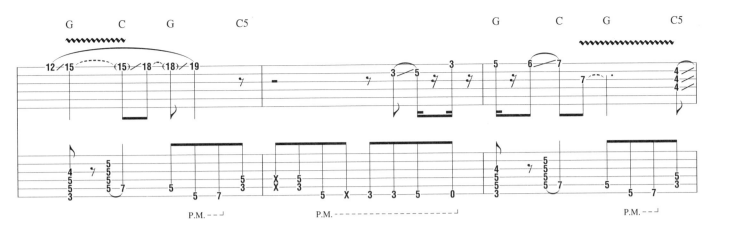

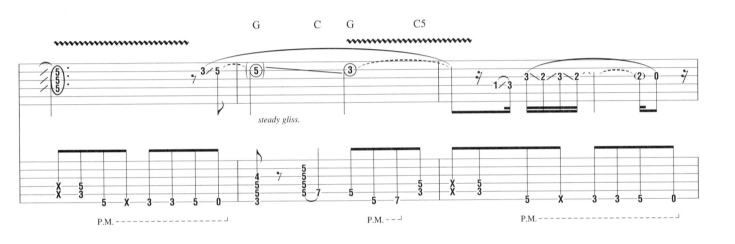

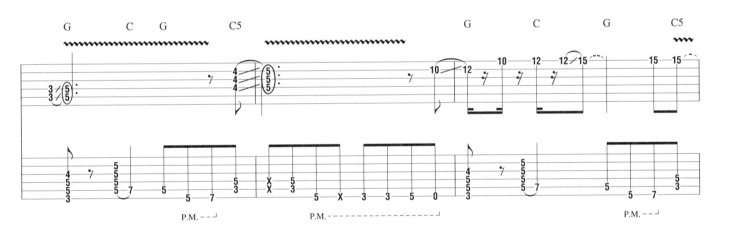

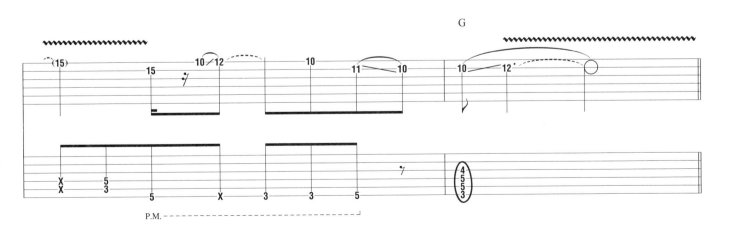

MORE DOUBLE STOPS

Double stops using 4ths or 6ths (a note that is harmonized with another note that is the interval of a 4th or a 6th away) are very effective in standard-tuned slide playing because they can approximate the sound of a guitar tuned to an open chord. The following G major pentatonic licks employ double stops using either 4ths or 6ths.

 Double Stops – Lick 1

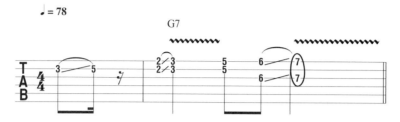

 Double Stops – Lick 2

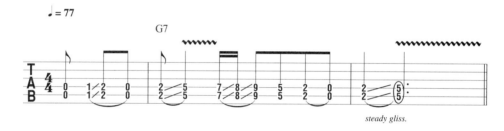

steady gliss.

 Double Stops – Lick 3

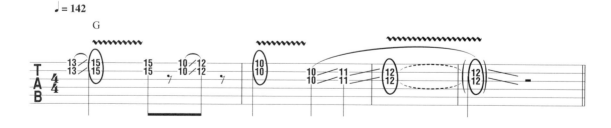

 Double Stops – Lick 4

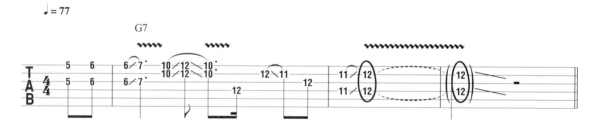

VOLUME SWELLS WITH DOUBLE STOPS

Playing double stops or triple stops with volume swells can give them a haunting, soulful sound like a steel guitar. To perform a volume swell, use the pinky on your picking hand to cradle the volume control on your electric guitar. Start with the volume rolled off, then pick the desired notes and bring the volume up immediately after. Here is an example:

 Volume Swells – Lick 1

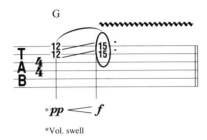

Here are some G major pentatonic licks using double stops and volume swells. You can also position the slide diagonally on the fretboard so that part of the slide is a half step (one fret) away from the other part of the slide, allowing you to get a major 6th double stop, as in the second example below.

Volume Swells – Lick 2

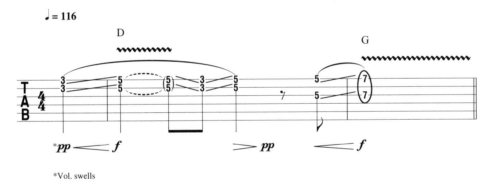

Volume Swells – Lick 3

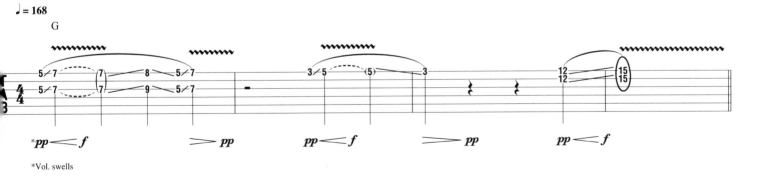

25

The following is a tune utilizing double and triple stops, volume swells, and all the other goodies in our toolbox that we've learned thus far. The chord progression is a I–vi–ii–V vamp with a bridge that goes: IV–I–IV–I–IV–I–ii–V. Over the vi and ii chords, we can play double stops, and on the IV chord, we can arpeggiate a triple stop that contains the ♭7th, 9th, and 5th of C9 and sounds quite effective. I am also bringing our moveable blues positions to the party, along with the major pentatonic scale. Here 'tis:

 Steelin' in G

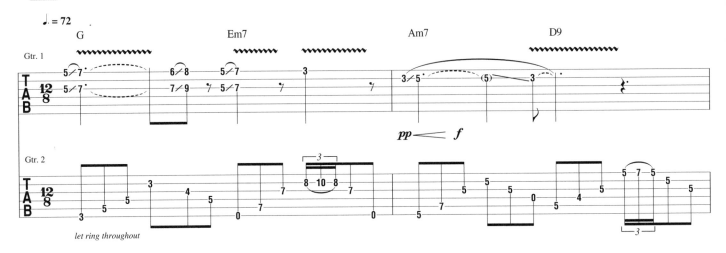

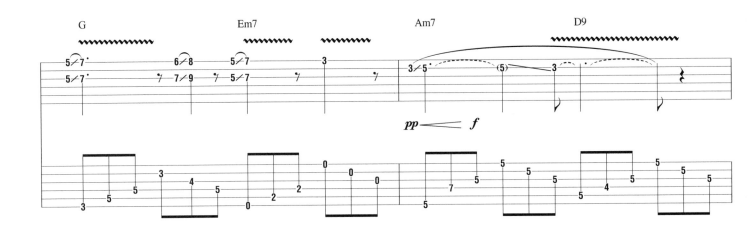

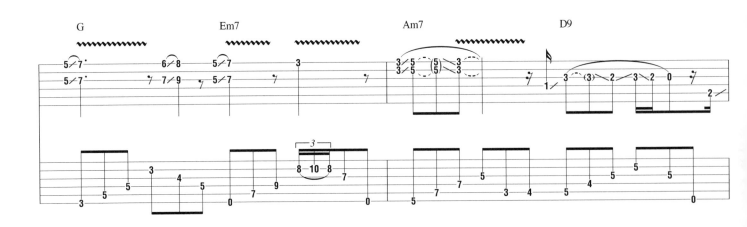

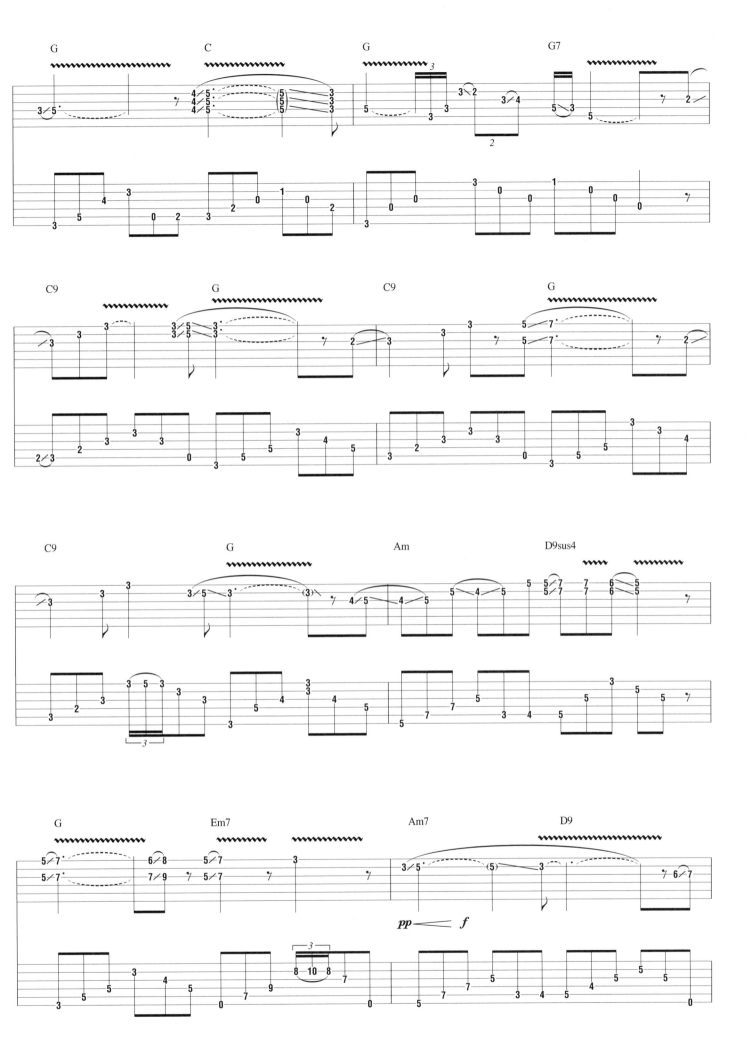

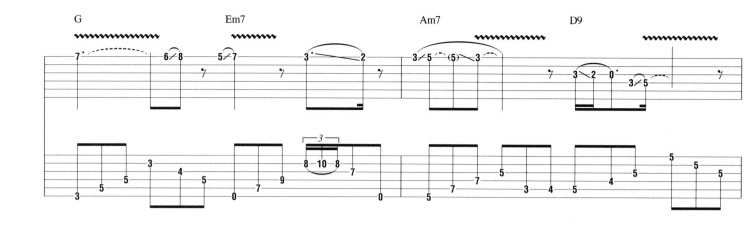

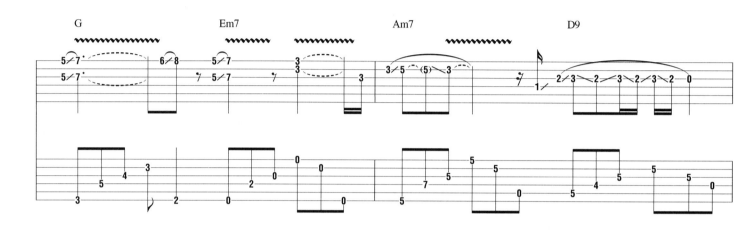

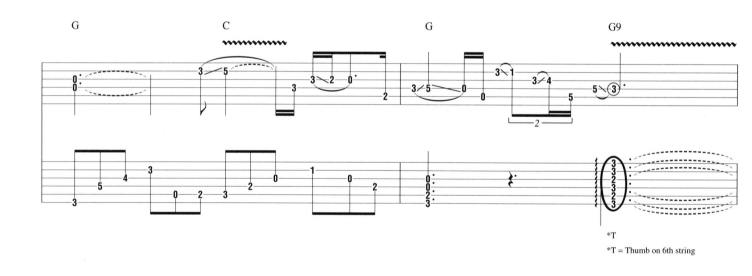

*T

*T = Thumb on 6th string

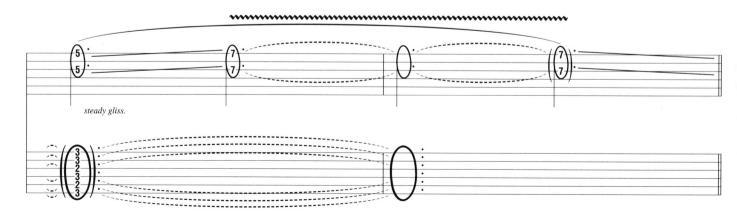

steady gliss.

Adding More Color Tones

In addition to the ♭3rd, we can incorporate a couple more effective color tones to our major pentatonic improvisations. When playing over the I chord, you can add the major 7th, like this:

 Color Tones – Major 7th

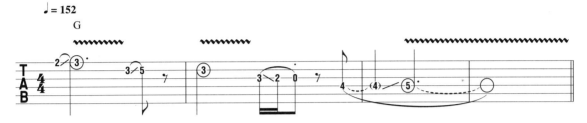

You can also add the 4th for a suspended quality that causes a pleasant tension and is quickly resolved to the major 3rd:

 Color Tones – 4th

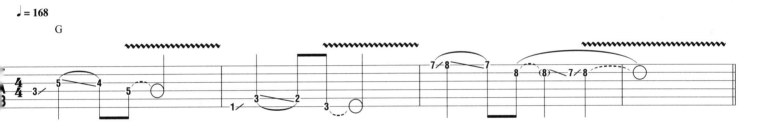

You can also add another passing tone to the major pentatonic scale. This time, it's a ♭6th, which adds a nice chromatic flow when running the scale:

 Color Tones – ♭6th

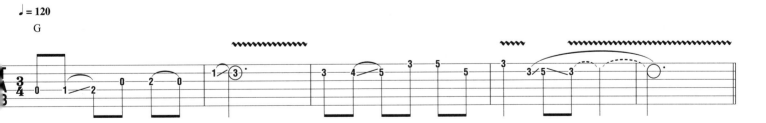

The following blues in G is going to employ our new color tones, as well as the full bounty of what we've learned so far.

Toolbox Blues

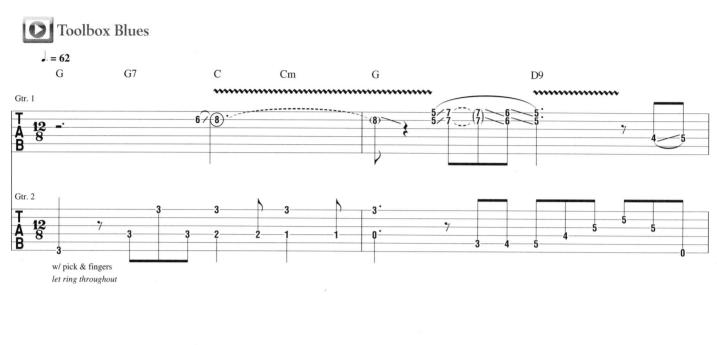

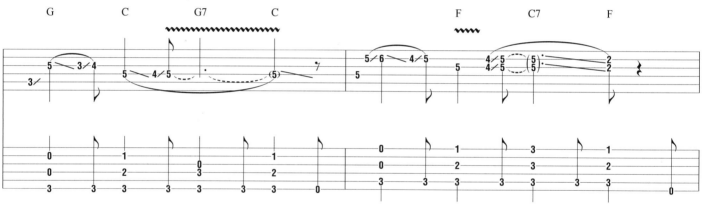

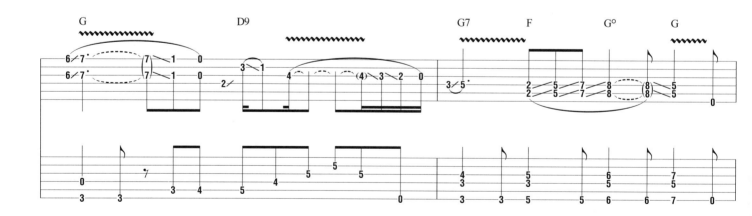

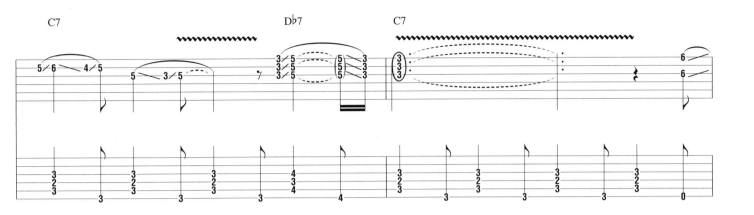

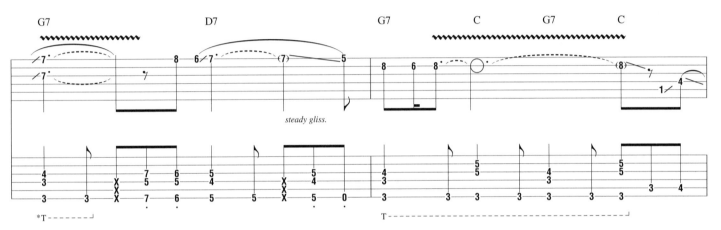

*T = Thumb on 6th string

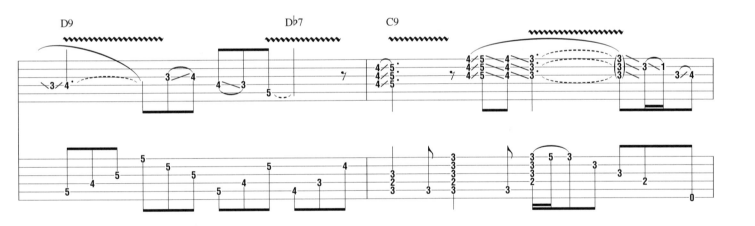

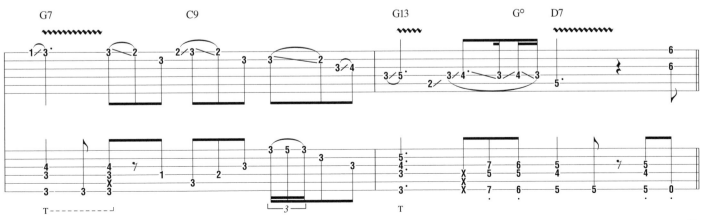

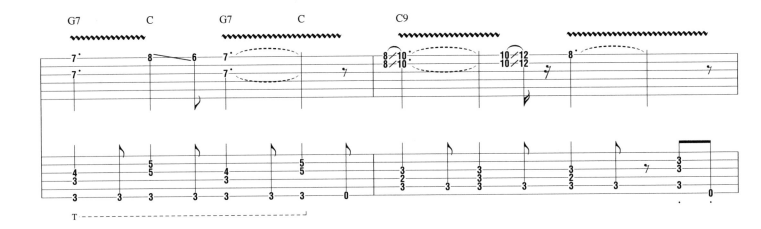

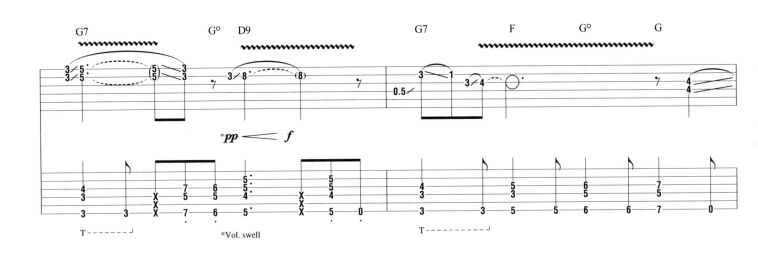

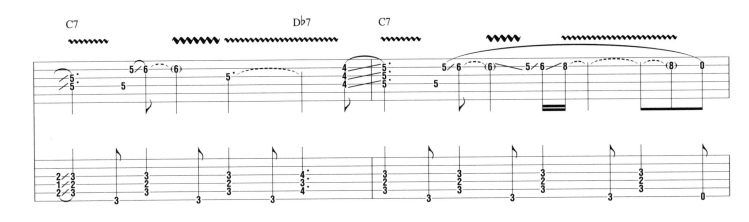

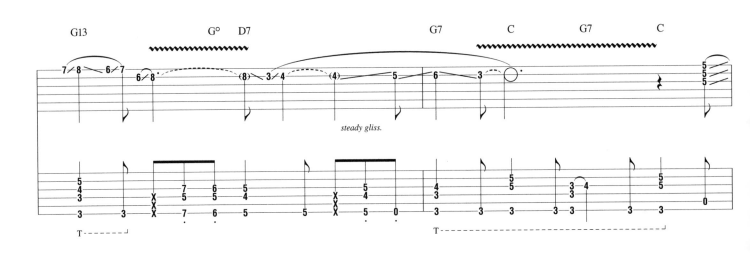

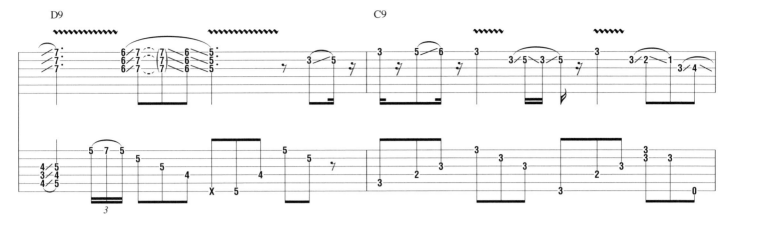

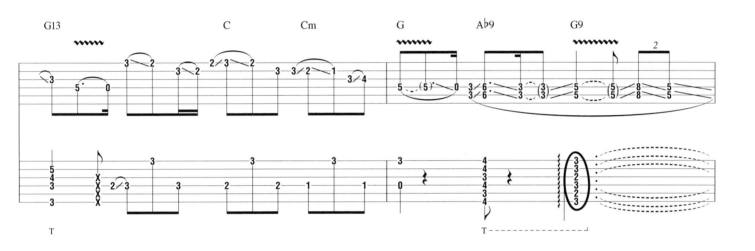

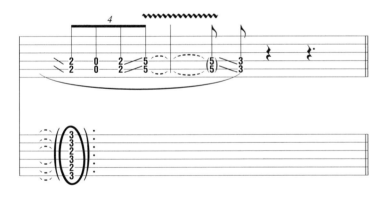

A LITTLE MORE EXOTIC

To get a little more exotic sounding when playing the blues, you can add some different flavors that sound even more exotic when playing slide. For instance, over a G major or G dominant seventh chord, if you play the C harmonic minor scale but with G as the root (G Phrygian dominant), you get a very spicy flavor indeed.

Let's run the scale, sliding up to each note both ascending and descending, and then try a couple of licks using the scale. I'll have a G11 chord going on behind the scale so you can hear how it works over that chord:

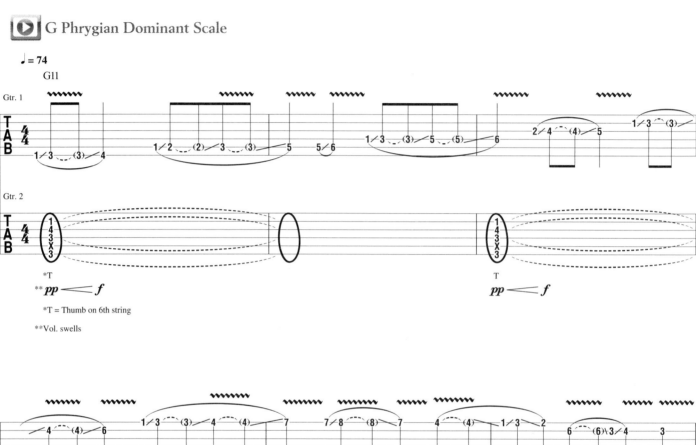

*T = Thumb on 6th string

**Vol. swells

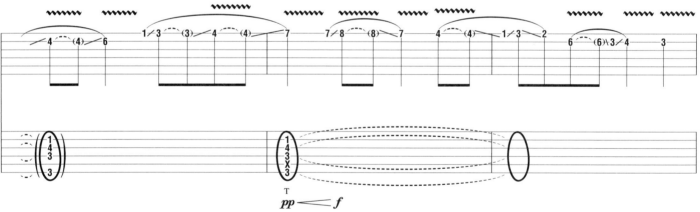

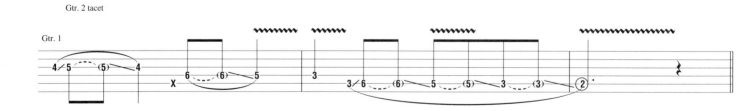

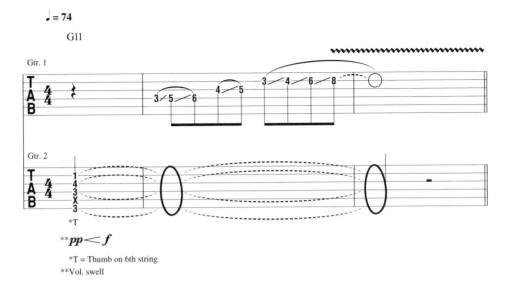

G Phrygian Dominant – Lick 1

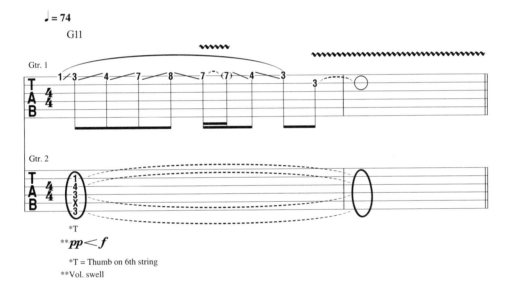

G Phrygian Dominant – Lick 2

THE FRETTED GLISSANDO

If you press down with the slide to the fingerboard, you can use the slide to fret notes to connected scale tones in a chromatic fashion, and the resultant glissando sounds really cool. You must keep in mind that, when you go back to using your slide in the normal fashion, you must adjust to being over the target fret wire instead of behind it, or your intonation will be off. Here's a basic example:

Fretted Glissando

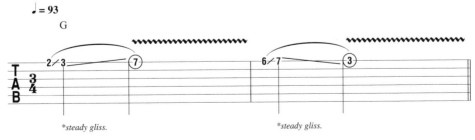

Now let's hear what it sounds like using our Phrygian dominant scale. Here are some lick examples:

▶ Fretted Glissando – Lick 1

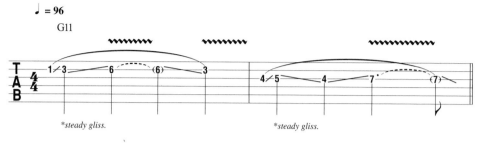

*steady gliss.

*Press slide down to fretboard while performing gliss.

▶ Fretted Glissando – Lick 2

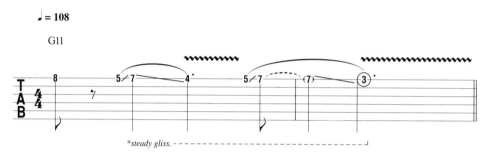

*steady gliss. -

*Press slide down to fretboard while performing gliss.

The following selection is a G7-based chord vamp that utilizes the Phrygian dominant scale, along with the fretted glissandos.

▶ Mysterioso Blues

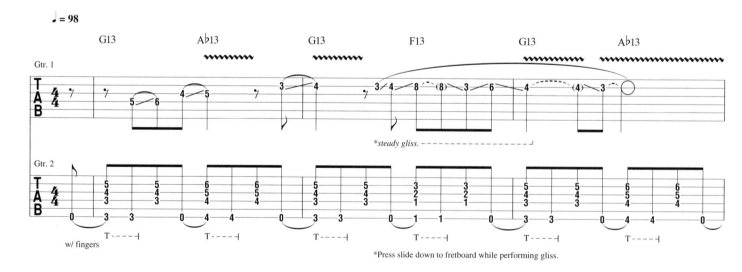

*steady gliss. - - - - - - - - - - - - - - -

w/ fingers

*Press slide down to fretboard while performing gliss.

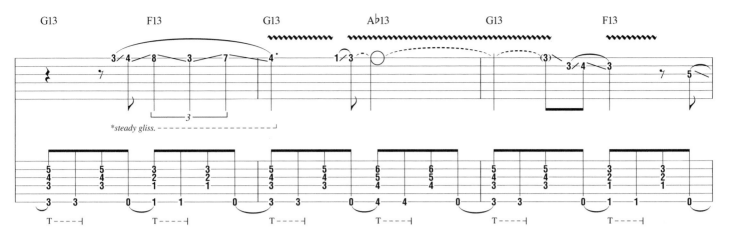

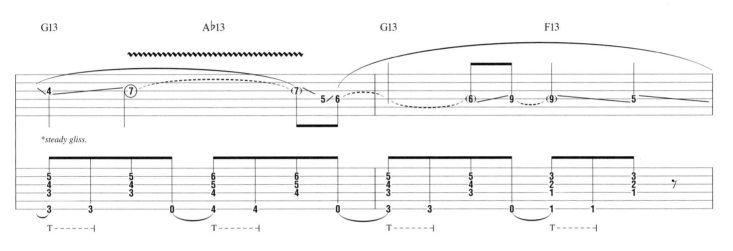

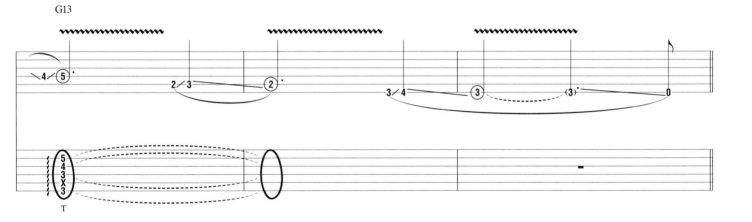

Minor Sliding

Playing over a minor chord as you improvise or perform fills with a slide can be done effectively by using just the blues scale. If you employ some double and triple stops, you can get some minor chord tones that are particularly effective. The following examples are for playing over an Am7 chord with the moveable blues scale position in the vicinity of the fifth fret.

Minor Sliding – Lick 1

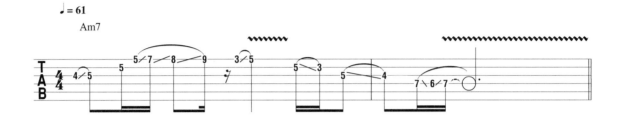

Minor Sliding – Lick 2

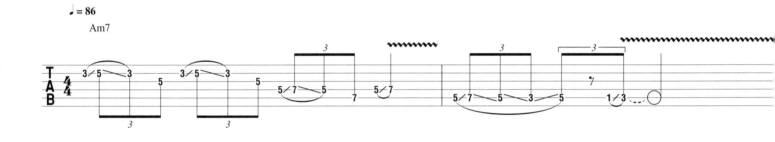

Minor Sliding – Lick 3

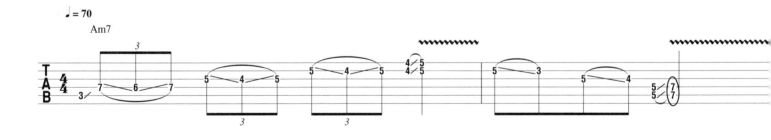

DORIAN MODE

Without getting into a full dissertation on the modes, I would at least like to reference using the Dorian mode as an effective tool for improvising over minor seventh chords, as well as for soloing over a blues. The A Dorian mode is comprised of the notes from the G major scale, but starting with A as the root; then you have the notes B, C, D, E, F♯, G, and back to A. The minor 3rd (C) and the minor 7th (G) make it a great fit for playing over an A minor seventh chord. Here is the scale descending and ascending in the same area of the neck as the previous moveable blues shape. I'm sliding up to each note and adding some vibrato here and there.

Dorian Mode

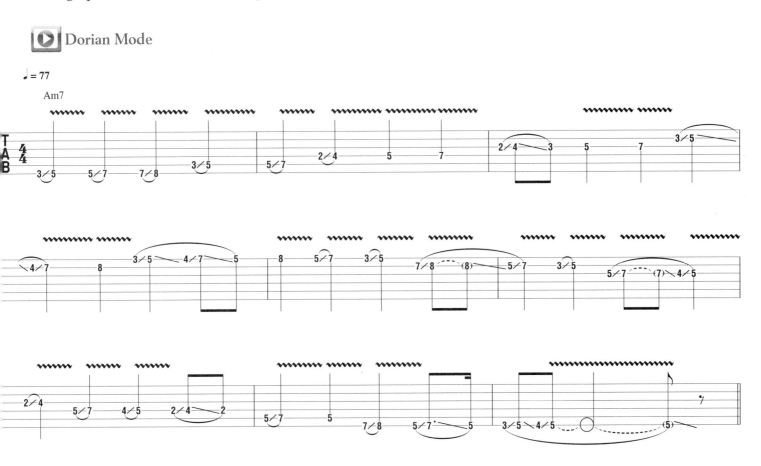

There are plenty of opportunities to use double stops with this scale, primarily with the intervals of 4ths, but there are minor 3rd double stops that are very effective, as well. Try it out with this exercise:

Dorian Mode with Double Stops

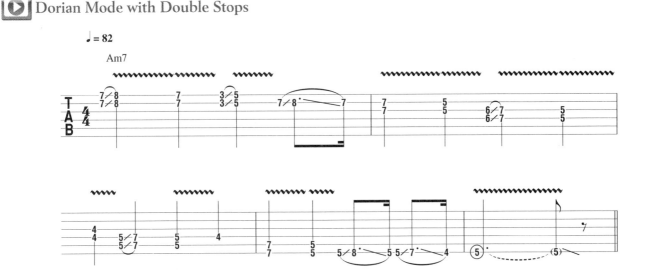

Let's try some triple stops using this scale. Some of these stacked 4ths voicings sound a little "out," but used in the right spirit, they can provide a cool flavor. The major and minor triads are very useful. Here are some examples of using these triple stops:

 Dorian Mode with Triple Stops

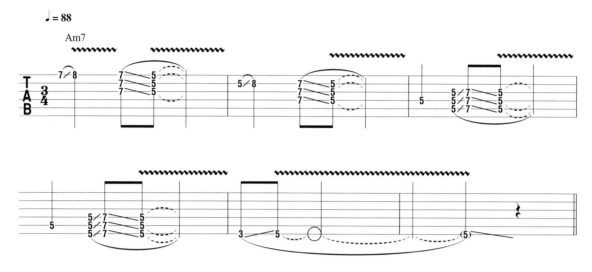

GOING HORIZONTAL: FRETTING BEHIND THE SLIDE

Knowing the friendly slide zones on the guitar neck is particularly useful, as you can slide up and down to great effect instead of adhering to a couple of positions. The following exercise goes up and down the neck with the A Dorian mode and harmonizes it with double stops on the B and high E strings. In order to make all the double stops adhere to the scale, we can lift up the slide slightly so that it is hitting the E string—but not the B string. You can then use the first or second finger on your fretting hand to fret the B string a fret or two away from where the slide is being used to achieve the desired intervals.

 Dorian Mode – Horizontal

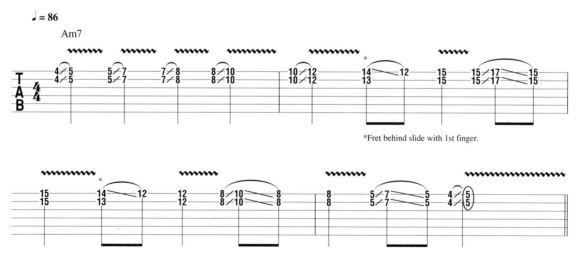

Here is one way that you can use these horizontal 4ths:

 Horizontal Lick 1

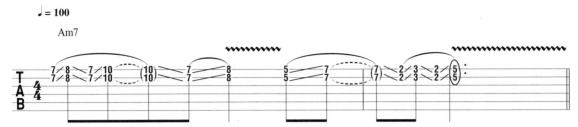

Now let's use the 4ths to harmonize the A blues scale as we run it horizontally on the B and high E strings:

 Horizontal Lick 2

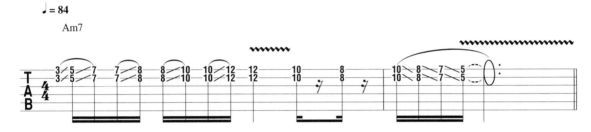

Here are some other ideas for how to use these:

 Horizontal Lick 3

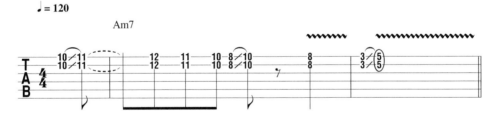

 Horizontal Lick 4

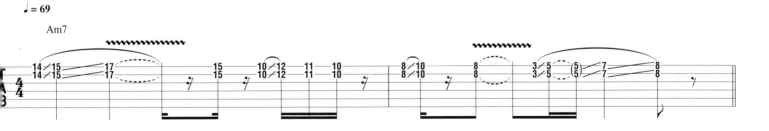

The following selection is an Am7–D9 vamp. The licks played utilize the A blues scale and the A Dorian mode. If you know your modes, you know that all the notes in A Dorian are the same notes as in D Mixolydian, and that is why it sounds "right" over the D9 chord. In addition to double and triple stops, you can also hear some of the fretted glissandos and other tools from our growing slide arsenal.

 Minor Vamp

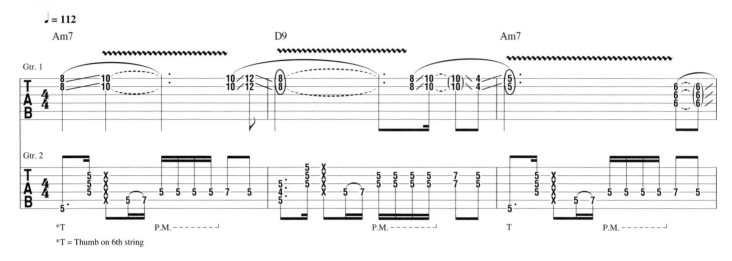

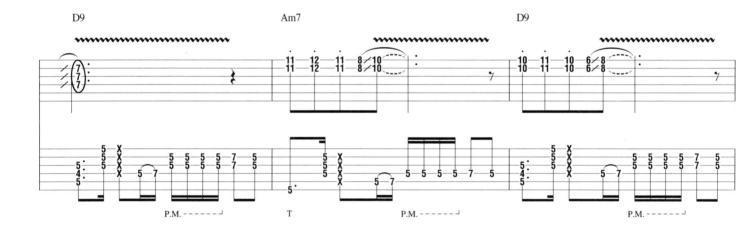

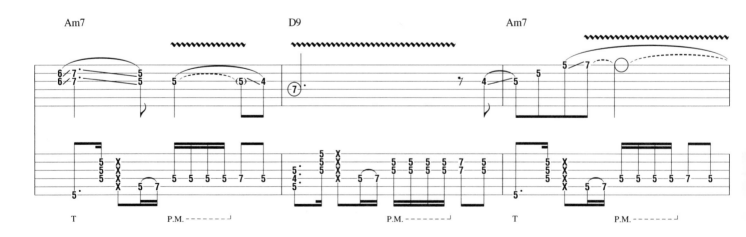

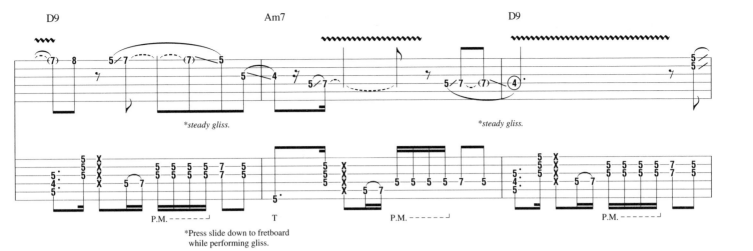

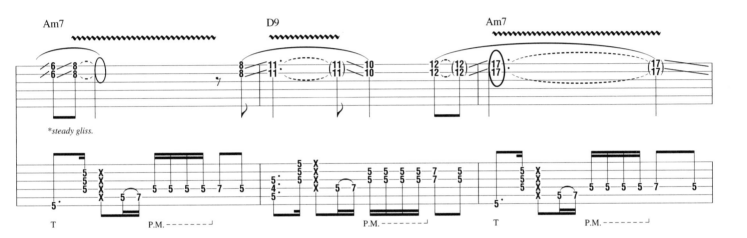

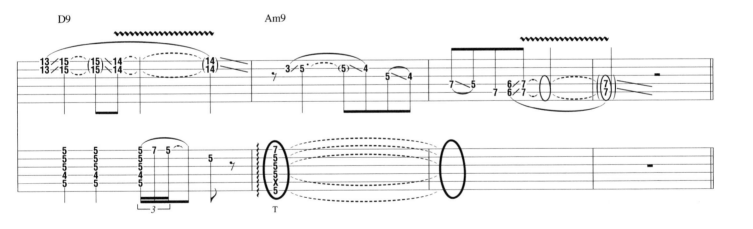

More Fretting Behind the Slide

A double-stop sound that you can achieve in standard tuning is one involving two notes that are a minor 3rd apart. To achieve this sound on the B and high E strings, you can use the slide to get the desired note on the B string while fingering a note two frets down on the E string. Then, lift the slide slightly so that you can hear both the fretted note and the slide note at the same time, like this:

▶ Fretting Behind the Slide

It is a little easier to intonate the two notes if you have more of a horizontal slant to both your finger and your slide.

Here are some licks using this technique in the key of E. Notice how adding vibrato to just the slide note makes it sound like you are adding vibrato to both.

▶ Fretting Behind the Slide – Lick 1

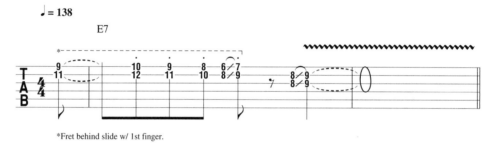

*Fret behind slide w/ 1st finger.

▶ Fretting Behind the Slide – Lick 2

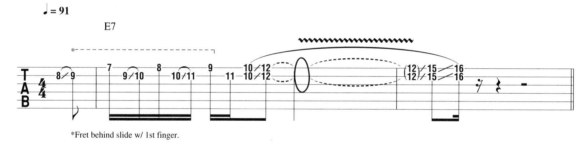

*Fret behind slide w/ 1st finger.

You can also alternate between using the slide on the high E string and lifting it to hear the fretted note behind it, like this:

▶ Fretting Behind the Slide – Lick 3

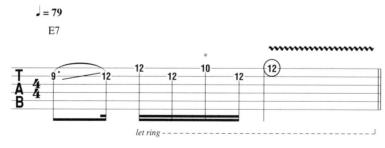

*Fret behind slide w/ 1st finger.

Here are some licks in the key of E that are played on the B and high E strings and use this technique:

▶ Fretting Behind the Slide – Lick 4

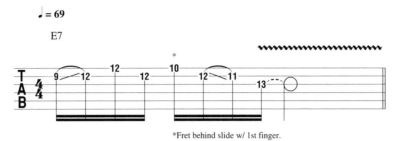

*Fret behind slide w/ 1st finger.

▶ Fretting Behind the Slide – Lick 5

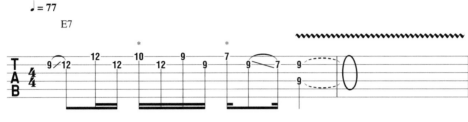

*Fret behind slide w/ 1st finger.

You can also use this technique on other adjacent strings. If we do it with the G and B strings, the notes of the minor 3rd double stop are only one fret away from each other. Again, a slightly horizontal hand placement makes these two notes easier to intonate. The following licks use double stops on the D and B and G and B strings, respectively:

▶ More Fretting Behind the Slide (0:00)

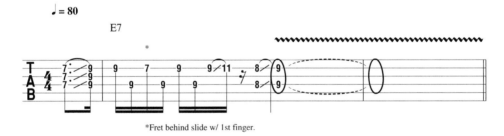

*Fret behind slide w/ 1st finger.

▶ More Fretting Behind the Slide (0:20)

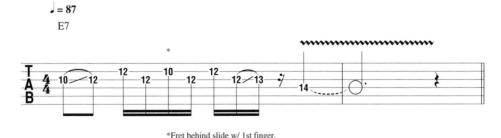

*Fret behind slide w/ 1st finger.

The following example is a blues in E that utilizes "fretting behind the slide" double stops, along with other things we have learned thus far.

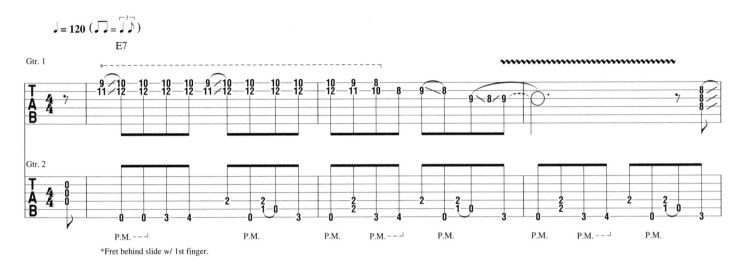

Frettin' and Slidin' Blues

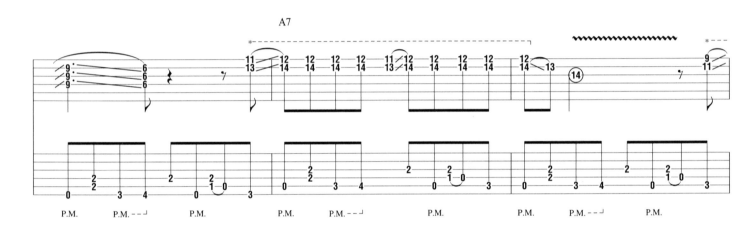

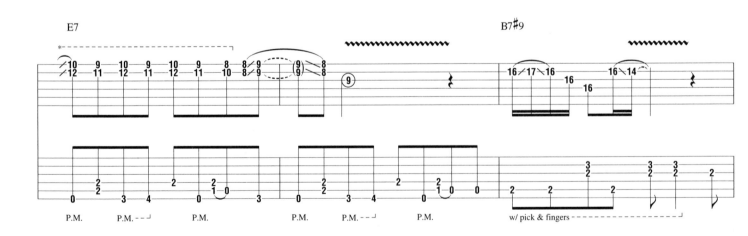

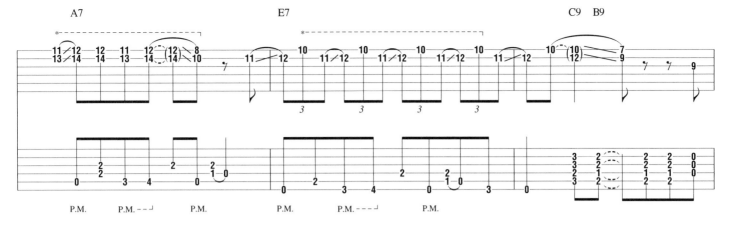

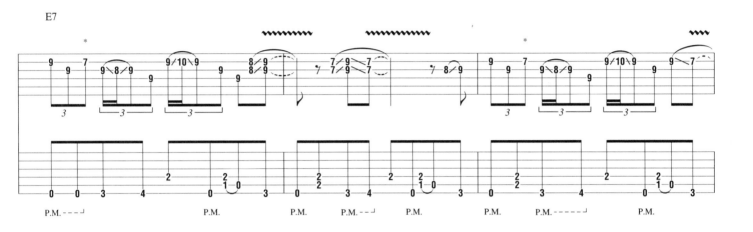

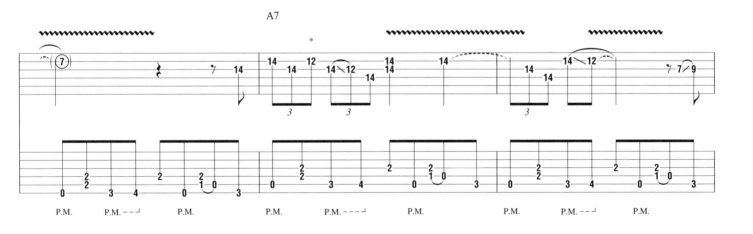

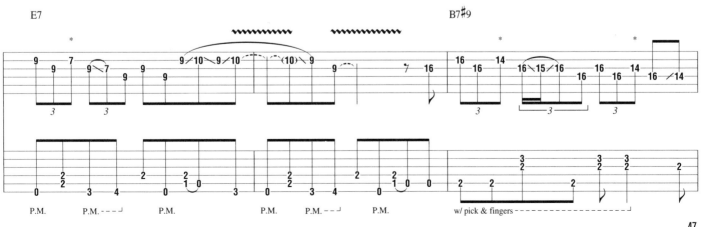

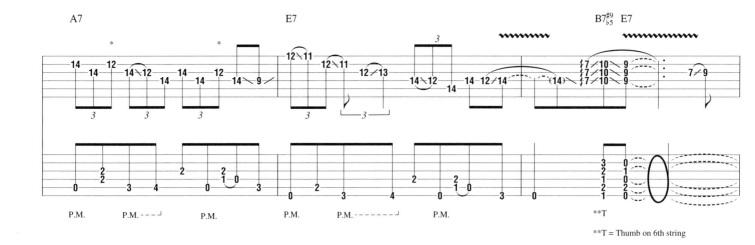

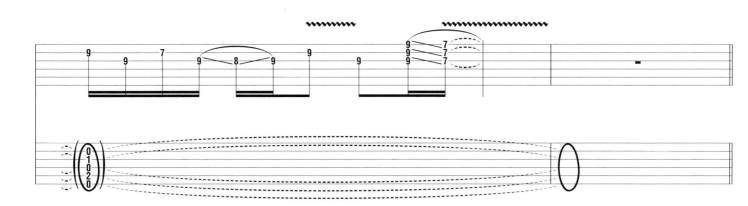

Harmonic Sliding

A technique that is used to great effect by lap-steel and pedal-steel players is picking a harmonic 12 frets up from where the slide is resting on the strings, and then once the harmonic note sounds, you can bring the slide up the neck while a ghostly harmonic changes pitch as you do so. In order to pick the harmonic with the picking hand, you can rest your first finger over the string, 12 frets up from where the slide is resting, and then pick the note, either with another finger or with a pick that is being held by your thumb and middle finger. Once the note sounds, you move the slide up the neck. Here is an example on the high E string:

 Harmonic Sliding

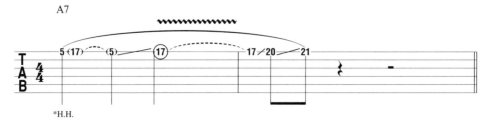

*Using the pick-hand index finger, touch string 12 frets above slide fret and pluck string with pick-hand ring finger or thumb

Wrapping It All Together

Before we do one last piece that uses a little bit of everything we have learned, let's take a look at a few variations on some techniques.

PEDAL-STEEL SOUNDS

We can get a pedal-steel-type effect by using the "fretting behind the slide" technique. In this example, you can achieve an ascending, pedal-steel-sounding run by hitting a fretted note and then hammering down on the same string with the slide, and then doing the same thing using multiple strings.

 Pedal-Steel Sounds – Lick 1

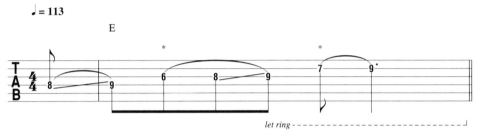

*Fret behind slide and hammer on with slide.

This next example uses the slide diagonally on the fretboard to achieve double stops that give you a pedal-steel-type sound.

 Pedal-Steel Sounds – Lick 2

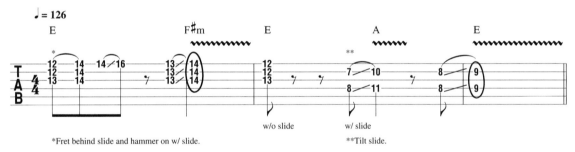

DIMINISHED SOUNDS

You can accentuate a diminished chord by playing double stops using 6ths that ascend or descend every four frets. These can be done on the D and B strings or the G and high E strings. Here's how these work over a diminished chord:

 Diminished Sounds

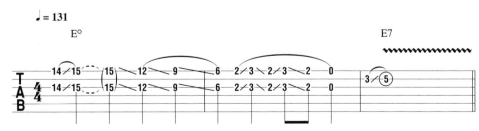

This closing selection features a little bit of almost everything we have learned throughout the course of this book. It is in the spirit of the gospel steel players who went on to influence the likes of Robert Randolph and Derek Trucks. It is in the key of E, but the chords move around so that minor and diminished ideas, along with blues and major pentatonic flavors, are all present.

 **Churchy Steel**

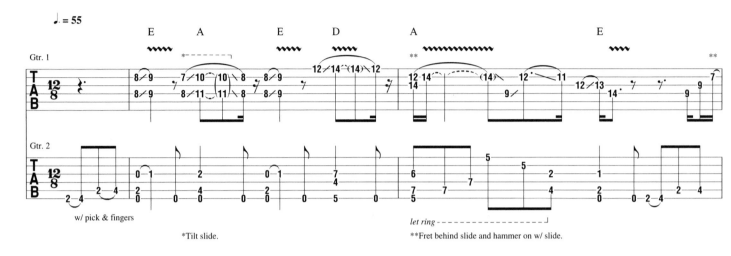

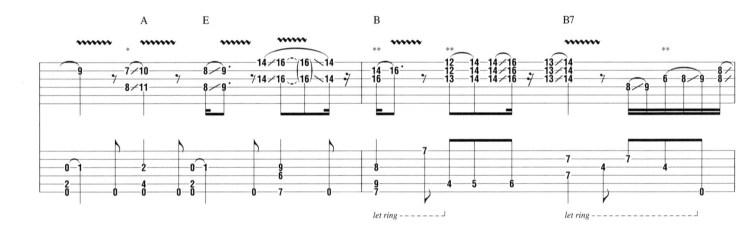

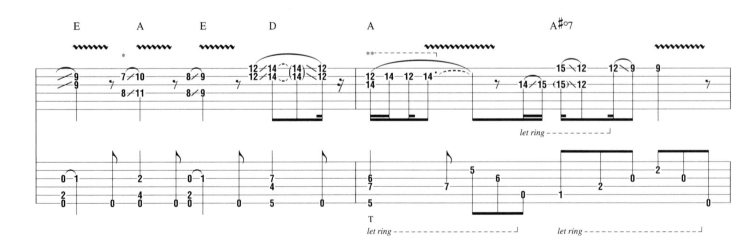

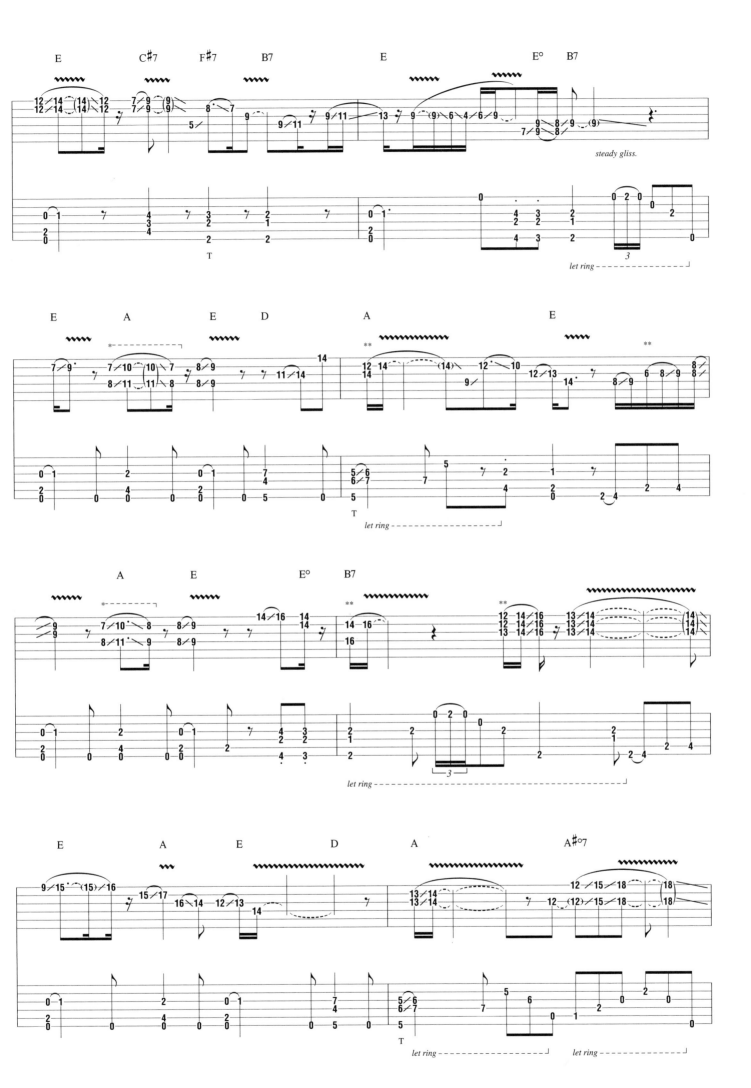

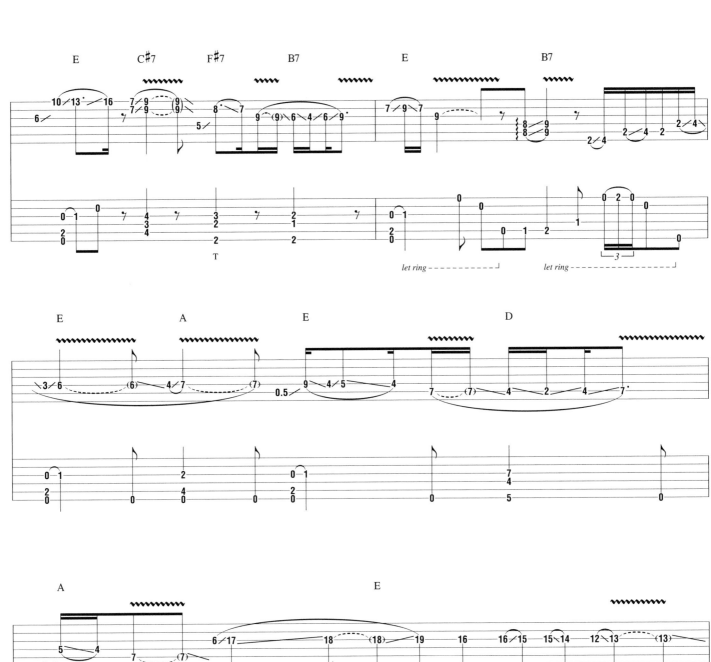

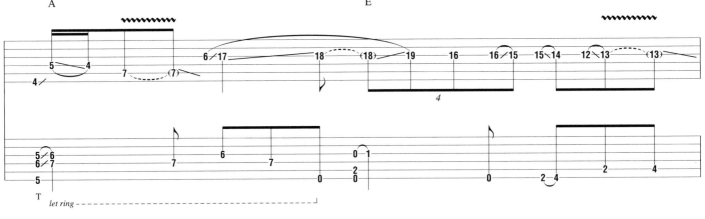

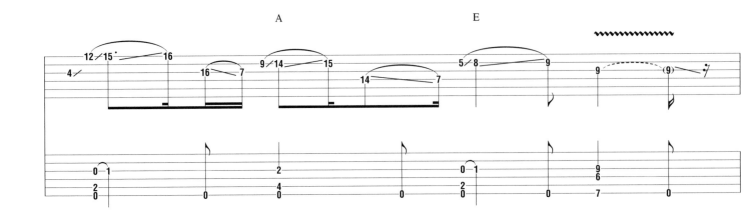

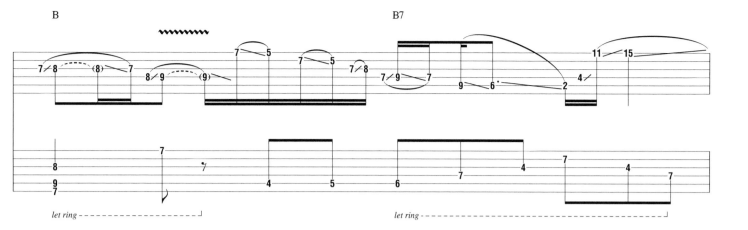

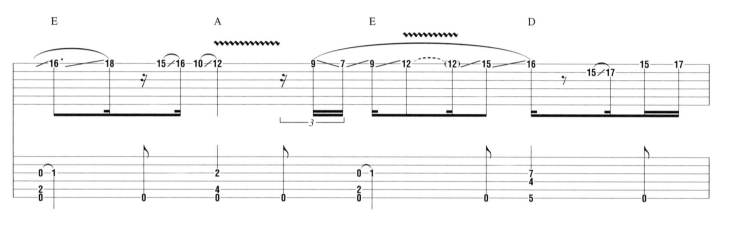

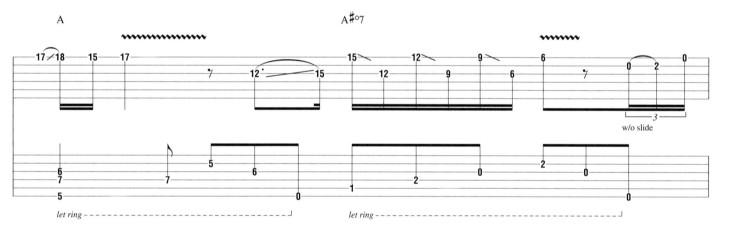

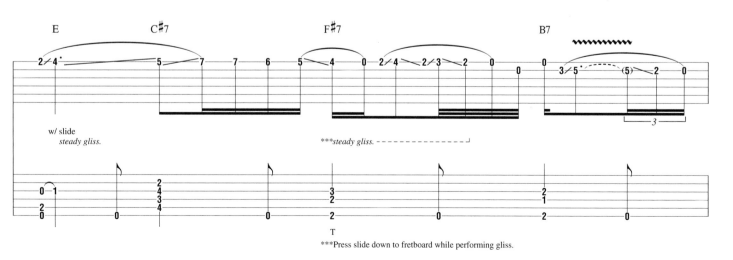

***Press slide down to fretboard while performing gliss.

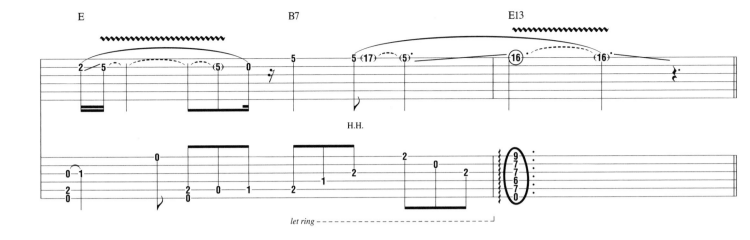

I hope you have learned a lot and that you are inspired to continue your quest for slide guitar excellence!

Rhythm Tab Legend

Rhythm Tab is a form of notation that adds rhythmic values to the traditional tab staff.

TABLATURE graphically represents the guitar fingerboard. Each horizontal line represents a string, and each number represents a fret. Rhythmic values are shown using ovals, stems, and dots.

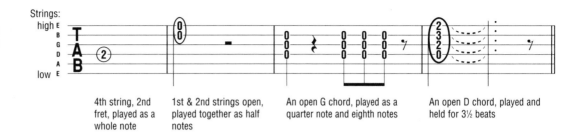

| 4th string, 2nd fret, played as a whole note | 1st & 2nd strings open, played together as half notes | An open G chord, played as a quarter note and eighth notes | An open D chord, played and held for 3½ beats |

DEFINITIONS FOR SPECIAL GUITAR NOTATION

HALF-STEP BEND: Strike the note and bend up 1/2 step.

WHOLE-STEP BEND: Strike the note and bend up one step.

GRACE NOTE BEND: Strike the note and immediately bend up as indicated.

SLIGHT (MICROTONE) BEND: Strike the note and bend up 1/4 step.

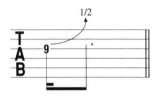
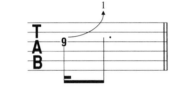
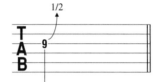
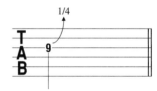

BEND AND RELEASE: Strike the note and bend up as indicated, then release back to the original note. Only the first note is struck.

PRE-BEND: Bend the note as indicated, then strike it.

PRE-BEND AND RELEASE: Bend the note as indicated. Strike it and release the bend back to the original note.

UNISON BEND: Strike the two notes simultaneously and bend the lower note up to the pitch of the higher.

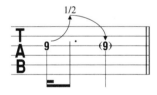

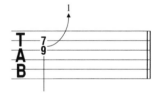

HOLD BEND: While sustaining bent note, strike note on different string.

VIBRATO: The string is vibrated by rapidly bending and releasing the note with the fretting hand.

WIDE VIBRATO: The pitch is varied to a greater degree by vibrating with the fretting hand.

HAMMER-ON: Strike the first (lower) note with one finger, then sound the higher note (on the same string) with another finger by fretting it without picking.

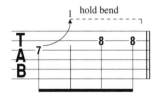

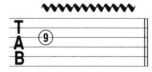
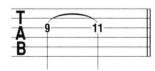

PULL-OFF: Place both fingers on the notes to be sounded. Strike the first note and without picking, pull the finger off to sound the second (lower) note.

HAMMER FROM NOWHERE: Sound note(s) by hammering with fret hand finger only.

GRACE NOTE SLUR: Strike the note and immediately hammer-on (or pull-off) as indicated.

GRACE NOTE SLUR (CLUSTER): Strike the notes and immediately hammer-on (or pull-off) as indicated.

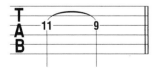
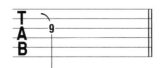

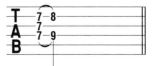

LEGATO SLIDE: Strike the first note and then slide the same fret-hand finger up or down to the second note. The second note is not struck.

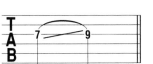

SHIFT SLIDE: Same as legato slide, except the second note is struck.

TRILL: Very rapidly alternate between the notes indicated by continuously hammering on and pulling off.

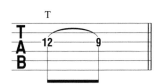

TAPPING: Hammer ("tap") the fret indicated with the pick-hand index or middle finger and pull off to the note fretted by the fret hand.

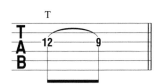

NATURAL HARMONIC: Strike the note while the fret-hand lightly touches the string directly over the fret indicated.

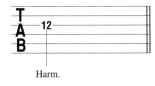

PINCH HARMONIC: The note is fretted normally and a harmonic is produced by adding the edge of the thumb or the tip of the index finger of the pick hand to the normal pick attack.

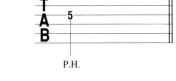

HARP HARMONIC: The note is fretted normally and a harmonic is produced by gently resting the pick hand's index finger directly above the indicated fret (in parentheses) while the pick hand's thumb or pick assists by plucking the appropriate string.

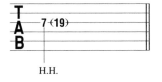

PICK SCRAPE: The edge of the pick is rubbed down (or up) the string, producing a scratchy sound.

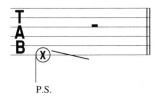

MUFFLED STRINGS: A percussive sound is produced by laying the fret hand across the string(s) without depressing, and striking them with the pick hand.

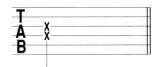

PALM MUTING: The note is partially muted by the pick hand lightly touching the string(s) just before the bridge.

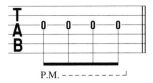

RAKE: Drag the pick across the strings indicated with a single motion.

TREMOLO PICKING: The note is picked as rapidly and continuously as possible.

ARPEGGIATE: Play the notes of the chord indicated by quickly rolling them from bottom to top.

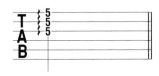

VIBRATO BAR DIVE AND RETURN: The pitch of the note or chord is dropped a specified number of steps (in rhythm), then returned to the original pitch.

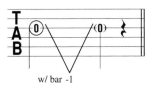

VIBRATO BAR SCOOP: Depress the bar just before striking the note, then quickly release the bar.

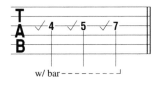

VIBRATO BAR DIP: Strike the note and then immediately drop a specified number of steps, then release back to the original pitch.

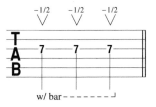

ADDITIONAL MUSICAL DEFINITIONS

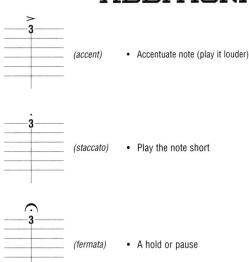

(accent) • Accentuate note (play it louder)

(staccato) • Play the note short

(fermata) • A hold or pause

⊓ • Downstroke

∨ • Upstroke

• Repeat measures between signs

NOTE: Tablature numbers in parentheses are used when:
- The note is sustained, but a new articulation begins (such as a hammer-on, pull-off, slide, or bend), or
- A bend is released.

56